KITCHEN FUN

Teaches children to cook successfully

Louise Price Bell

DERRYDALE BOOKS
New York • Avenel

This edition is published by Derrydale Books,
distributed by Random House Value Publishing, Inc.,
40 Engelhard Avenue, Avenel, New Jersey 07001.

Random House
New York • Toronto • London • Sydney • Auckland

Printed and bound in the United States

Library of Congress Cataloging-in-Publication Data
Bell, Louise Price.
    Kitchen fun / by Louise Price Bell.
    Summary: Presents a collection of recipes for candy, cakes, cookies, salads,
and vegetables.
    ISBN 0-517-66927-7

    1. Cookery – Juvenile literature. [1. Cookery] 1. Title
TX652.5.B43 1988   88-10951
641.5'123 – dc19   CIP
                                                                        AC

10 9 8 7 6

Foreword

There is nothing more comforting than the rich smells and the warmth generated in your kitchen. It is a safe and happy place where good cooking leads to delicious meals and happy memories. Hot cocoa on a long, wet afternoon, freshly baked gingerbread ready for dinner's dessert, and warm breakfast biscuits straight from the oven all remind us of our childhoods, and we remember how eagerly we learned the secrets of good cooking from our parents, grandparents, and older brothers and sisters.

In *Kitchen Fun* classic recipes of childhood have been brought back to teach a new generation of children how to cook successfully and with enjoyment. They will enjoy preparing—and eating—Southern Cornbread, Cinderella Cake with Jam Frosting, Spicy Applesauce, Yummy Eggs, Circus Salad, Uncooked Fudge, and the absolutely *best* Chocolate Milk ever. All these recipes let children be real cooks, yet are easy to follow and never so advanced as to cause frustration or kitchen disaster. Complete with Rules For Little Cooks, a Table of Measurements, and an illustrated ingredients list for each recipe, *Kitchen Fun* easily lives up to its name.

It is impossible not to be inspired by this collection—young cooks will want to hurry out to the kitchen to use these recipes. Adults will also want to share this cook book with the children in their lives— nieces, nephews, grandchildren, sons, daughters, and young friends, introducing them to successful recipes that will lead to kitchen competency and lifelong skills.

New York   Anne James

1988

CONTENTS

Bran Muffins

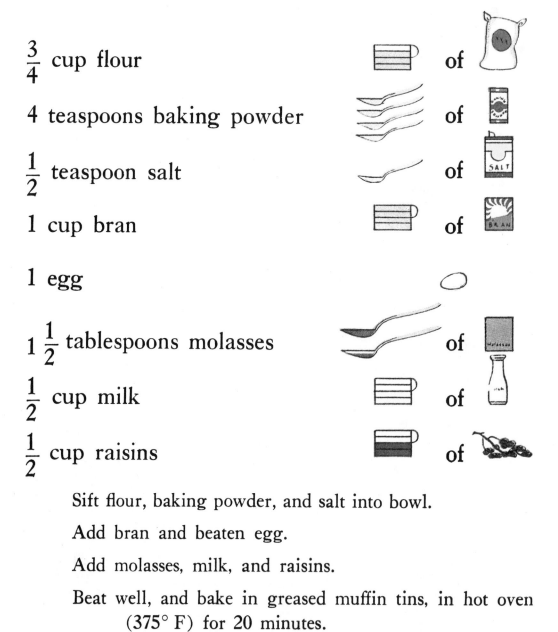

$\frac{3}{4}$ cup flour

4 teaspoons baking powder

$\frac{1}{2}$ teaspoon salt

1 cup bran

1 egg

$1\frac{1}{2}$ tablespoons molasses

$\frac{1}{2}$ cup milk

$\frac{1}{2}$ cup raisins

Sift flour, baking powder, and salt into bowl.

Add bran and beaten egg.

Add molasses, milk, and raisins.

Beat well, and bake in greased muffin tins, in hot oven (375° F) for 20 minutes.

Southern Corn Bread

$\frac{1}{4}$ cup sugar

2 tablespoons butter

1 egg

1 cup milk

1 cup flour

$\frac{3}{4}$ cup corn meal

4 teaspoons baking powder

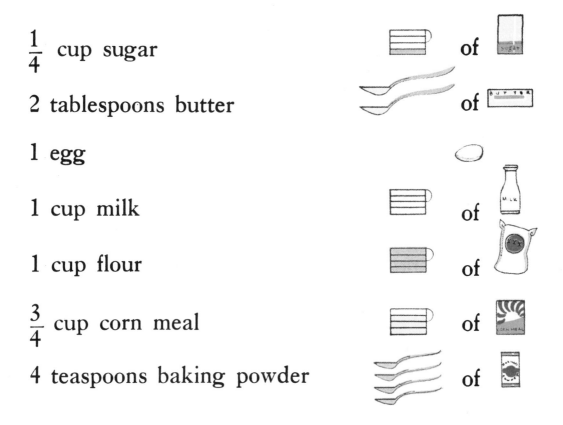

Cream the sugar and butter in a bowl.

Beat egg, then add egg and milk.

Sift flour, corn meal, and baking powder, and add.

Beat well, and bake in shallow, greased pan in moderate oven (350° F) for 45 minutes.

Party Biscuits

2 cups flour

4 teaspoons baking powder

1 teaspoon salt

4 tablespoons butter

$\frac{2}{3}$ cup milk

Sift flour, baking powder, and salt into bowl.

Mix butter in with knife or fingers.

After butter is well mixed, add milk slowly.

Roll dough out on floured board.

Cut with biscuit cutter.

Bake on greased baking sheet in hot oven (375° F) for 15 minutes.

Peanut Butter Cookies

$\frac{1}{4}$ cup sugar

2 tablespoons butter

$\frac{1}{2}$ cup peanut butter

1 egg

2 tablespoons milk

$\frac{1}{2}$ cup flour

1 teaspoon baking powder

$\frac{1}{2}$ teaspoon salt

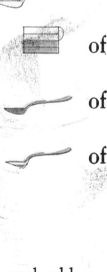

Cream sugar and butter in a bowl.

Add peanut butter, and beat well.

Beat egg, and add, then add milk.

Sift flour, baking powder, and salt, and add.

Beat well.

Drop with spoon on greased cookie sheet, and bake in hot oven (375° F) for 15 minutes.

7

Chocolate Nut Drop Cookies

1 cup sugar

$\frac{1}{4}$ cup butter

1 egg

$\frac{1}{2}$ cup milk

1$\frac{1}{2}$ cups flour

2 teaspoons baking powder

$\frac{1}{2}$ cup cocoa

1 cup nut meats

Cream sugar and butter in a bowl.

Beat egg, and then add the egg and milk.

Sift flour, baking powder, and cocoa, and add to mixture, then add nuts. Stir well.

Drop with spoon on greased baking sheet and bake in hot oven (375° F) for 15 minutes.

8

Fairy Gingerbread

1 cup sugar

$\frac{1}{2}$ cup butter

2 eggs

1 cup milk

1 cup molasses

$2\frac{1}{2}$ cups flour

$\frac{1}{2}$ teaspoon soda

1 tablespoon ginger

Cream sugar and butter in a bowl.

Beat eggs, then add eggs, milk, and molasses.

Sift flour, soda, and ginger into mixture and beat well.

Bake in shallow greased pan in moderate oven (350° F) for 45 minutes.

9

Cinderella Cake

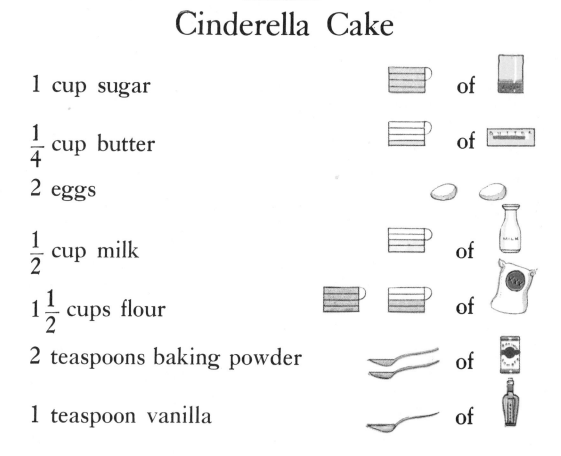

1 cup sugar

$\frac{1}{4}$ cup butter

2 eggs

$\frac{1}{2}$ cup milk

$1\frac{1}{2}$ cups flour

2 teaspoons baking powder

1 teaspoon vanilla

Cream sugar and butter in a bowl.

Beat eggs, then add eggs and milk.

Sift flour and baking powder and add.

Add vanilla and bake in greased cake tin in moderate oven (350°F) for 45 minutes.

When cool, frost with Jam Frosting. (page 11)

Jam Frosting

4 tablespoons raspberry jam   of

1 teaspoon water   of

1 cup confectioner's sugar   of

Put jam in saucepan on stove.

Stir over low heat until jam is melted.

Add water.

Remove from stove.

Sift confectioner's sugar and add.

Beat hard, and spread carefully on Cinderella Cake.
(page 10)

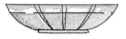

Spicy Apple Sauce

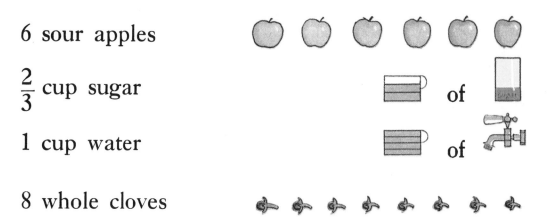

6 sour apples

$\frac{2}{3}$ cup sugar   of

1 cup water   of

8 whole cloves

Wash apples.

Cut apples in quarters.

Take out core carefully.

Put apples, sugar, water, and cloves in saucepan.

Cook $\frac{1}{2}$ hour slowly.

Mash through colander or strainer.

Rainbow Dessert

2 cups boiling water   of

1 package raspberry gelatin

2 bananas

2 oranges

3 slices canned pineapple

Pour boiling water on gelatin in bowl.

Stir until gelatin is all dissolved.

Peel bananas and oranges.

Cut pineapple, oranges, and bananas in small pieces.

Add fruit to gelatin, and pour into mold.

Cool, then put in refrigerator.

Serve plain or with whipped cream.

Tapioca Pudding

2 cups milk

1 $\frac{1}{2}$ tablespoons minute tapioca

2 eggs

$\frac{1}{3}$ cup sugar

1 teaspoon vanilla

Heat milk and tapioca in double boiler.

Stir often.

Beat eggs, then mix eggs and sugar.

Stir egg mixture into tapioca, slowly.

Cook and stir until thick or about 15 minutes.

Let cool, then add vanilla.

Serve plain or with cream.

Rice Whip

1 cup whipping cream

$\frac{1}{2}$ cup sugar

1 cup crushed pineapple

2 cups cooked rice

Whip cream until stiff, then add sugar.

Mix pineapple and rice carefully.

Add the whipped cream and mix well.

Serve very cold.

A red cherry on top of each dish looks very pretty.

Fudge Sauce

$1\frac{1}{2}$ cups sugar

1 cup cocoa

1 cup water

1 teaspoon vanilla

Mix sugar, cocoa, and water in pan.

Boil 15 minutes.

Cool, then add vanilla.

This is delicious over ice cream, cake, or pudding.

Chocolate Milk

1 glass milk  of

1 tablespoon fudge sauce
   (page 16) of

Stir the sauce into milk.
Serve with soda straw.

Hot Chocolate

1 cup milk of

1 tablespoon fudge sauce
   (page 16) 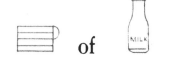 of

Heat milk in saucepan.

Stir in fudge sauce.

Serve hot with marshmallow on top.

Yummy Eggs

4 eggs

1 cup milk   of

$\frac{1}{2}$ teaspoon salt   of

1 tablespoon butter   of

Beat eggs until light and foamy.

Add milk and salt, and beat.

Add butter and put in double boiler.

Cook over boiling water in double boiler for 20 minutes.

Baked Salmon Loaf

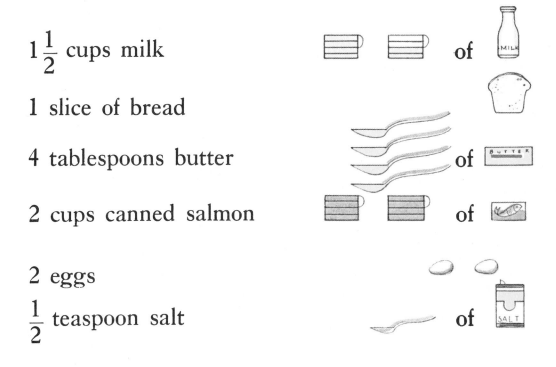

$1\frac{1}{2}$ cups milk

1 slice of bread

4 tablespoons butter

2 cups canned salmon

2 eggs

$\frac{1}{2}$ teaspoon salt

Heat milk, bread, and butter in double boiler until creamy.

Remove bones from salmon carefully.

Beat eggs, and mix with salmon, salt, milk, bread, and butter, stirring well.

Bake in greased bread pan in moderate oven (350°F) for 1 hour.

Serve hot or cold.

Old King Cole Spinach

2 eggs

2 cups cooked spinach  of

Beat eggs until foamy.

Chop spinach fine, in chopping bowl.

Mix spinach and eggs well.

Pour into buttered baking dish.

Bake in moderate oven (350°F) for $\frac{1}{2}$ hour.

Surprise Carrot Loaf

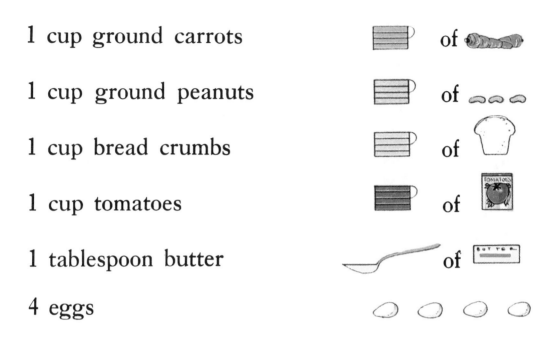

1 cup ground carrots

1 cup ground peanuts

1 cup bread crumbs

1 cup tomatoes

1 tablespoon butter

4 eggs

Grind carrots, peanuts, and bread through food chopper.

Add tomatoes and butter, and mix well.

Beat eggs until foamy, then add.

Bake in greased bread pan in moderate oven (350° F) for
    1 hour.

Circus Salad

3 oranges

$\frac{1}{2}$ cup shelled peanuts

Animal crackers

Lettuce

Peel oranges, and cut in small pieces.

Chop peanuts fine in chopping bowl.

Mix oranges and peanuts.

Fill little lettuce cups with salad.

Put animal crackers around edge of plate, and one on top of salad.

Choo-Choo Salad

4 large raw carrots

1 cup raisins   of

1 tablespoon orange juice   of

Lettuce

    Grind carrots and raisins through food chopper.

    Mix with orange juice.

    Serve on crisp lettuce leaf.

Chocolate Fudge

2 cups sugar   of

$\frac{1}{2}$ cup cocoa   of

1 cup milk   of

2 tablespoons butter   of

1 teaspoon vanilla   of

Put sugar, cocoa, milk, and butter in saucepan.

Mix well.

Cook for 15 minutes, slowly.

Remove from stove and beat hard, until creamy.

Add vanilla.

Pour into shallow buttered pan to cool.

When cool cut in squares.

Uncooked Fudge

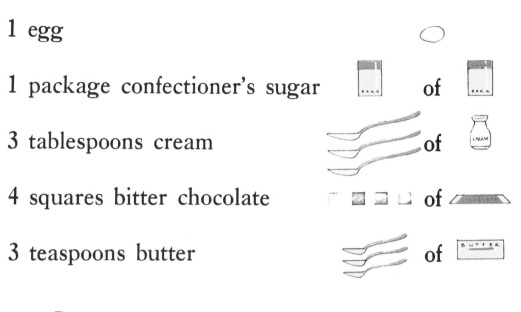

1 egg

1 package confectioner's sugar

3 tablespoons cream

4 squares bitter chocolate

3 teaspoons butter

Beat egg.

Stir 1 cup of sugar into egg.

Add cream.

Stir in rest of sugar.

Melt chocolate and butter in top of double boiler over boiling water.

Add to sugar, egg, and cream.

Spread in tin and cut in squares.

Penuche

2 cups brown sugar

$\frac{2}{3}$ cup milk

3 tablespoons butter

1 cup nut meats

$\frac{1}{2}$ teaspoon vanilla

Mix sugar, milk, and butter in saucepan.

Cook for 15 minutes, slowly.

Remove from stove.

Add nuts and vanilla and beat until creamy.

Pour into shallow buttered pan to cool.

When cool cut in squares.